POETRY AND STORIES FROM A WORKING CLASS MIND

To ALISON

Love DAVID

Published in paperback in 2021 by Sixth Element Publishing
on behalf of David Randall

Sixth Element Publishing
Arthur Robinson House
13-14 The Green
Billingham TS23 1EU
www.6epublishing.net

© David Randall 2021

ISBN 978-1-914170-03-4

British Library Cataloguing in Publication Data. A catalogue record for this book is available from the British Library.

All rights reserved. No part of this publication may be reproduced, stored in a retrieval system or transmitted, in any form or by any means, electronic, mechanical, photocopying, recording and/or otherwise without the prior written permission of the publishers. This book may not be lent, resold, hired out or disposed of by way of trade in any form, binding or cover other than that in which it is published without the prior written consent of the publishers.

David Randall asserts the moral right to be identified as the author of this work.

Printed in Great Britain.

This work is a work of creative non-fiction. Some of the work is based on real life, but some of the names, characters, organisations, places, events and incidents portrayed are either products of the author's imagination or are used in a fictitious manner.

POETRY AND STORIES FROM A WORKING CLASS MIND

DAVID RANDALL

Contents

A note from the author 1
Introduction 3
Diamond in the womb 4
Swapping a lock knife 6
Crossing the path of evil 7
Pulling out the eyes of prejudice 13
Rocks in our chests 15
Comfortably blind 16
The wolf and the old Indian 17
A man's home is his castle 18
Fields of conkers 19
Mental note to a stranger 20
A jester in an angel's hand 21
Tears in front of the TV 23
Seaweed and heartstrings 25
Let's all breed thugs 34
I pushed her away 35
Hallelujah when chosen 36
Green velvet eyes 37
Broken kings 39
A burning sensation 40
Sydney and Stella 41
Honesty and fear 45
Mothers of the world 46

Peacock dresses for the Chinese twins	47
Lost reflections	50
The devil's smile	51
Holding another man	53
Clocks keep ticking	54
Eating hope for breakfast	55
So it's not just me	56
Upsetting the gods	57
Miniature screwdrivers	58
Oceans of frost	59
I asked her to hold me	62
Zombie apocalypse	63
Holding on to your honour	64
The Stag Inn	65
Souls of new beginnings	67
Coffee and whisky in the staffroom	68
Smile with me	70
Confusions of the stupid ones	71
Moving through the swill	72
The Parmesan bandits	73
Hunger for everything	78
Do you really want to suffer?	79
Open your eyes	80
The innocent ones	81
Self-forgiveness is trapped in the fist of a bronze statue	82

To the stars and back	84
Stuff it	85
Stephen's freedom	86
Dementia	87
The love boat	88
A strange breed	89
The labourer	90
Finding it	95
Broken records	96
Puddles, olives, perfume and the purse	98
Words that hurt, words that heal	111
Enjoying the solitude	112
Planet eyeball	113
I have no spare change	115
The fly in the soup	117
A heart in a bed of nettles	118
Pennies or sweets	119
Spinning letters	120
The vermin in the rain	121
Empty cabin	122
Buckets of glitter	123
Let's be realistic	124
Shopping list	125
Cream	126
Digging in the mud	127

I can't cope	128
Lights out	129
Hitchhiker's guide to the funny farm	130
Unwanted games	138
The adventures of Captain Onion	139
Stop saying that	141
A tight grip	142
Future through a monster's eye	143
Sobriety	145
Cuckoo	146
Think about it	147
Endless friendships	148
Strong seeds	149

A note from the author

I've worked since I was 14 and I grew up fast around real men and women. Strong people, positive and hard working class people.

I've seen extreme violence.

I've seen and felt extreme love.

I think life has led me to this book to tell others they are not alone.

I'm 42 now and have my own company. I still get up and work really hard because that's how I will always be. But the hard work is also in myself. I suffer from agoraphobia, an anxiety disorder which has kept on me for twenty years, and also depression. But it is a long fight but there will only be one winner, one still standing... ME.

I see life as art.

You just have to open your eyes and be better to each other...

I wrote this book for people to stay positive and carry on in life.

It is hard but also easy and beautiful at times.

Basically it doesn't matter if you don't feel good enough or even if you fail,

What matters most is that you are trying your best.

One day when you won't expect it.

Life will rub you gently on the cheek and say,

"Hey, you are going to be okay."

Introduction

For all the bin men who
take away the postman's
rubbish
Who ties his bootlaces
and delivers
with a whistle and a smile
The bricklayers
Plasterers
Plumbers
The little old lady in the
café who takes so long
making my breakfast
every morning
And to all those who get
out of bed to do an honest
day with self respect
In their hearts.

Diamond in the womb

To the bump in the belly
To the smile upon the face
To hard grips of parents' hands
To the birth they both embrace
To feed on the breast of life and innocence
Soothing new characteristics as he grows
He looks like father
He looks like mother
Kept safe and warm
This is a new diamond
Born into the universe
And she will be the perfect mother
Soon he will crawl, reaching for the shelf
Not being able to keep his tiny fingers to himself
Mother will want to stop time and keep things this way forever
But laws of nature do not work like this
The first day at school
The shoelace lesson
The packed lunch made with mother's love
Small note to tell him so
Toys will turn to comic books
Comic books will attract a best friend to adventure with
He will walk the streets with his black dog
He will whistle tunes
He will look up at the stars

Mother will make food and await her diamond
He will blush but will still kiss the girl
He will get frustrated at his mother
But will soon be sorry and say so
For he and his mother are one
He came from her womb and part of his heart still remains there
One day he will have whiskers and a job
Then one day mother will have another diamond placed into her arms
One day mother will become grandmother
She will still feel the power of the love and will see beauty again through older eyes
And the circle of life will carry on into a fountain of embrace until her end
And she will have always been mother.

Swapping a lock knife

All I needed as a child was a cornfield to venture.
The summer sun.
A cold drink of water from the council tap.
To stroke my dog and rub his belly.
And the warm love of a working class family.

Crossing the path of evil

I just can't sleep
It doesn't matter how hard I try
My mind is just racing
It just will not switch off
Thought after thought
Pictures in my mind
Old memories
Distant conversations
I turn and switch on my little lamp
It's bright
I close my eyes
Maybe I can sleep with it on
But no it's just not going to happen
So I pick up my book
Find the page and start to read
This is no good either it just makes
My eyes sore
Okay fuck it, I say,
And just get up
I walk into the kitchen and put
On the light
My two little dogs are in their bed
One is hanging halfway out
They both look at me and I smile
Wakey wakey, kids,
I say
They jump up expecting to go out

NO, I say loudly
I make a cup of tea and sit on my sofa
Their little faces are just watching me
Okay okay, I say and put my coat on
Maybe some fresh air will make me sleep,
I say to them
We walk from the house and they want
to piss up every single thing in sight
I just have to stand there and watch
We walk across the field
Into the old churchyard
One of my dogs is about to cock his leg
Up against a gravestone
NO, I shout
Then grab him
I look at the gravestone
I try to read it
But it has long ago warn out its name
A forgotten soul, I say
To my little friends
We walk on
The dogs both stop
I try to pull them but they just drag
Their paws
Like statues scraping across the ground
Their necks are choking so
I stop pulling
I crouch down and stroke them
What the fuck is wrong? I ask them

I stroke them again
I try to comfort them
They are both trembling hard
It's worrying me
They are not looking at me
They are looking past me
I turn slowly
I see a man standing there
He makes me feel strange and unsettled
He has on an old worn out tuxedo
It is very dirty
Round the stomach where it seems
to have a yellow rim
It's pitted and seems to have red stains all over it
It looks like blood
His hair is slicked back like a sort of old
Teddy boy type of style
It is greasy black and thick
He looks at me and smiles
I do not smile back
His teeth are sharp and pale green
He then raises his hand and
Takes a smoke from a cigarette
It burns hard with a pointy end
Like a pyramid on fire
His nails are long and stained with nicotine
I can see he bites them
They are jagged
He smiles again at me

I still do not smile back
I feel uneasy
I'm very uncomfortable
I see he has something in his other hand
But it is dark
It appears to be a leather leash
He twists it around his dirty hand
Tightly
I see a strange figure is in the shadows
I try to see it and squint my eyes to do so
It seems he is walking something
It looks strange
Twisted thin and ugly
I step closer but can't figure out why
He smiles again and takes another drag
Blows a smoke ring
While all the time staring at me
I step closer again only this time I smell
A foul decaying stench
I gag and put my hand over my mouth
My eyes water
Then he smiles again
From the shadowy pit
Next to the man's leg
I see a thin hand wrap around it
Then I see its eyes looking at me
They are light blue
I can see its body is brittle and unnourished
The smell is unbearable

Its face comes more into
The light of the distant moon
I look down at it
It seems to have a small mark under its nose
It has hair but that is also black and greasy
It screeches at me with a disturbing noise
I feel sick and pale
I am frozen like my dogs
But yet I still move closer
The man's eyes are shiny pink holes
Like oyster pearls
But not kind
More threatening
The creature leaps up towards me
To protect its master
I am unable to step back
The man yanks at the leash
The creature flies back and crashes to
The ground on its side
As the man drags it back by its neck
Its arms and legs spread
It is bleeding and marked
Bruises and open wounds
I see it is naked and has a cock
I see it is so filthy it is almost black
He then kicks the creature
In the face
It gargles on its blood
Then it lets out a loud shriek

A sound so desperate
My hairs on the back of my neck stand up
The man takes a last drag of the cigarette
And flicks it at me
It lands next to my foot
I look down at it burning its last
Then I look back up
He is not smiling anymore
He kicks the creature again in the ribs
It yelps in agony
Let's go, boy
He says in a low voice
Then he spits at it
It lands on the creature's back
Amongst all the dirt
They walk off into the night
As the creature walks on all fours
It looks back at us
I see the wide blue eyes
The small mark under its nose
Seems to be black
And square shaped.
Adolf Hitler was Satan's lapdog
And was always destined to be.

Pulling out the eyes of prejudice

Why do we look at people with dwarfism
And find it so funny?
How do they agree to us letting it
seem so charming?
People call them midgets
Did you know that calling a person
with dwarfism a midget
Is like calling a black person a nigger?
And that is so so foul
Both words make me want to vomit
It makes me want to stop the world and get off
I walk out of places if I hear these words
Before I get too angry
No that's the wrong word
It's more psychopathic
I wish I was a black dwarf sometimes
I would lift weights
I would grow a giant beard
And a big handlebar moustache
I would have a big tattoo across my face from my
forehead down to my cheek over my eye
I'd have a big cigar and a gold tooth
I would be wild and outrageous
I would figure out the people
Who sniggered at me and pointed
Then I would smile and charm their wives
I would pull out my cock and swing it for their

husband or boyfriends to see
With the shock I'd smile
I would let out a great laugh with my slaver
dripping from my smoke
I would carry a blade
A cut throat razor
I would make them uncomfortable
And take away the humour
And spit in the face of ignorance
I would make them see
They are shallow and weak
And different from ME.

Rocks in our chests

It's easy to tell the youth of today
That they will move on
When they break up with a partner
You will find another boy
You will find another girl
You are still young
You must move on
You are being silly
We are the ones who are being silly
We are the ones who forget
We are the ones who let our hearts
be hardened from emotion
We are the ones holding up the shields
We should be ashamed
For forgetting
That love has no age.

Comfortably blind

I think a lot of people leave this earth
not knowing the answers.
But then there are so many that live
without questions.

The wolf and the old Indian

The king of the rats met with
the lord of the wolves
Why do you burrow through man's towns,
steal food and spread plague? asked the wolf
Why don't you? replied the rat
Because, said the wolf, a wise old Indian told me
that if we kept our distance and respected them
Then one day our name will be dog
Man will trust us
Feed us
Keep us close and warm
He lied, screamed the rat
No, said the wolf
I saw the truth in his eyes.

A man's home is his castle

I was sixteen and lying across the sofa
When it happened
I heard my grandad pull up
He walked his bike through the hallway
He walked in and took off his bicycle clips
My nana was sat on the floor near his chair
In front of the fire
He walked in all sweat
Beetroot red
He sat on his chair
With my nana sat below him
He then put his hands on her and said
Evelyn
I'd better die before you
Because I can't live without you
She looked round
They kissed
I learnt that day
The meaning of true love
I never wanted anything less for myself.

Fields of conkers

To be young and alive.
Ice cream from the van for all to enjoy.
Fields of conkers hear me weep.
Walnut whips and mam's Turkish delight.
Small whisky for nana at night.
Fields of conkers hear me weep.
Comedy on TV.
Sharing a bedroom with others.
No matching covers.
Fields of conkers hear me weep.
Compass and pen knife.
Different colours in the flashlight.
Horror movies.
Laughter and fright.
Fields of conkers hear me weep.
Cartoons in the morning.
Waiting for the new day.
Love was warming.
Fields of conkers hear me weep.

Mental notes to a stranger

Am I crazy? I say to the reflection.
Be quiet, you're okay, he tells me.

A jester in an angel's hand
(Gift of the sun)

Far away in the castle of face powder.
A place where laughter always grew louder.
But there is a place in this castle that
has been long forgotten.
A place nobody goes as it is so rotten.
In there sits a jester that has not been
given a name.
Left there in sadness, sorrow and shame.
Doing his tricks for the king and
using his false smile.
Just to entertain the wealthy
for such a short while.
Sitting eating his food on his straw mat.
And giving the crumbs to his only friend the rat.
Suddenly through the window
comes a beautiful great light.
So strong and so bright it almost takes his sight.
There stands a tall great angel.
He panics and wonders, has he lost his mind?
Could this be the madness
he thought he'd might find.
We give you the name HELIODORUS,
a name fit for a king.
Without silver or gold you are
no less human than him.
She takes him by the hand and flies him away.

To a wonderful great land and says he can stay.
The jester walks away from the angel, he walks
straight ahead.
The angel asks, what is this field
in which I have been led?
With tears in his eyes the jester crouches down
and this is what he said.
This is the moment I have longed to see.
As he opens his hands, the rat runs free…

Tears in front of the TV

I had a troubled youth at one point, not by my family's doing, just I got in with the wrong crowd. At the shock of how cruel the world could be, I took charge of my actions, and become responsible for them, because I knew that I was brought up by a hard-working-class proud family. And they deserved better than the way I was acting, and deep down inside it wasn't me. I come from good blood, and I knew better.

Afterwards, years later I was sat in a pub called the Falcon, and a very good friend of mine called Kevin McKitrick asked me how my grandad was doing. Suddenly I realised I'd been thinking of myself more than other people.

So I left my drink and I walked home. I saw the lights were off, but I saw that the TV was left on, and it warmed my heart because I knew my grandad was sat there watching telly as always. And that made me feel safe. I walked into the house and into the room. He was lying there on the sofa watching the telly.

I said, "Hey you, stand up," and he looked up at me, and said, "What?"

And I said, "Stand up."

He said, "No," and "What are you on about?" so he stood up.

He thought I was being silly and drunk, but I wasn't drunk.

So he just looked at me and smiled. The light was off, but the light off the TV made it clear for me to see his beautiful eyes. Gentle, kind, caring face. Everything a family man and a caring person should be; then I told him, "I've never ever told you how much I appreciate you bringing me up, and I love you so so much. You are my dad."

He looked at me with glassy eyes, and grabbed hold of me.

He squeezed me so much it hurt. He was a big strong man and I felt it. I then realised he had been waiting for them words. And I had become a man, and it was all because of him...

Seaweed and heartstrings

Size four Viking hooks was his choice, a good size hook for a good size cod. He could have used something a little bigger, but a decent size codling would do. It would do for the frying pan. And since Andrew's wife had left and was always complaining about the smell and stopping him from taking the fish home, now he told himself he could go back to that empty house and do whatever the fuck he liked. He had a couple of bags of squid in his bucket for bait. He had been given them off his friend Frankie who owned a fishing tackle shop in their town back home, and Frankie said to just pay for it when he could. Frankie had known that he was on hard times, but Andrew didn't like sympathy, and he was normally the one they asked if they needed anything. Frankie was a good friend, but not just that, he knew he couldn't just keep drinking pint after pint and it was making him numb and dragging him further down and making it harder to deal with. He needed to breathe and get away, needed space and time to think about what had happened in the last few weeks.

Fishing was something he was good at and had a passion for ever since he was a young boy. There was a seal sat at the steps at the bottom of the pier, looking up at him. It had big black sad eyes, he thought, and how they look a lot like dogs. If

I catch something I don't want. I'll throw it down there for it, if it's still there when I leave, he thought.

After being there for a couple of hours, he had already cast out a handful of times, but not a bite. He realised it had gotten dark quite quickly. Looking across into the town, it looked so tiny with it being so far away, but a few lights were still on. He carried on though as he got a nice big squid and wrapped it around his hook with the elastic string. It was a good job, he thought, and it would stay strong on the hook, stay solid in the water. It was getting windy but he cast as hard as he could, the rig flew strong and the line came out of the reel fast. But then it just stopped dead.

"THE FUCKING WIND," he shouted. "AAAH FUCK MY LIFE."

Andrew's face was burning even though it was cold, he was so angry, so pissed off. He reeled his line back in, and when it got half way back it had the biggest bastard wind knot in it.

"I give up," he said softly.

The annoyance of the tangled line overwhelmed him, and so he grabbed his knife and just cut the line. How easy, he thought, that it was to just cut away the pressure and see it just drift away into the wind.

A shadowy figure was walking down the steps of the old lighthouse. Andrew peeked for a second and at first he thought it was another fisherman, but it looked to be a man with a big white beard and a hat with curly white hair coming from the sides.

"Fuck me, it's Captain Birdseye." He looked away. It was the last thing he needed, some fella complaining about him climbing around the big steel gates to get in. It was off limits but he was alone and wasn't doing anybody any harm.

"You going to have a go at me for climbing around the gates, I suppose."

"That's not my job," the man said. "It's my job to guard the lighthouse not the gate at the bottom, and if you fall climbing round it, it's not my job to save you either."

"Who said I needed saving?" remarked Andrew.

The man struck a match and Andrew heard it strike, and thought the man must be an arsehole to try lighting a match in all this wind. He peeked at the man a little again and noticed a little red hole was burning as the man was holding a pipe to his mouth. "You must have climbed deep into your coat to manage that," he said.

But the man never answered and just carried on walking down to the bottom of the steps.

"Caught much?" the man asked.

"No," he replied, "but there's lights over there at the village, and I'm hoping it's a pub so I can just drink my arse to death."

The man laughed a little. "You will find more at

the bottom of that sea than you will at the bottom of a bottle, boy. Can I sit down here with you?" he asked.

"It's a big pier," Andrew replied, "but you can sit where you like."

The man sat down. "Not a lot of conversation around here is all."

"I wasn't really wanting one," Andrew said, but just as he did say it, he knew it sounded ugly and unkind. "Sorry," he said, and carried on looking across the sea.

"So what is your story, boy?"

Andrew was angry at him saying boy again, he wasn't a boy, he was 37 years old.

I'm not a fucking boy, he thought.

Andrew decided to just come right out with it, and probably make the man feel uncomfortable and just leave him alone.

"Well," he said, "my wife has left me and taken the kids. I've lost my job over the drink, but it's okay," he carried on. "She's with a new man called Nathan now, and Nathan has a great job offshore, and every time I get to see my kids it's Nathan this and fucking Nathan that. Can you help with that, do you think?"

The man was quiet and then replied, "Hmmm that's a tough cookie," and carried on smoking his pipe.

Cheeky bastard, Andrew thought and just shook

his head. "She's my wife and they are my kids," he said and his eyes filled up and his chin went into a shape like a walnut. "And I want them back."

"Sometimes you just can't have them back," said the man.

"Why not?" said Andrew.

"Because," the man said, "some things just slip away from you and we just can't control it. Life is hard but there's no point making it harder. It can be good too though and most can find it back through the other side."

"I'm trying," said Andrew. "I really am but it's just hard."

"Of course it's hard," the man said. "Life wasn't meant to be easy and that's the idea of it, that's the whole point. Love is like barnacles attached to the soul, boy, the grip is strong and can last a lifetime."

As Andrew's eyes filled up with tears, he still wouldn't look up at the man, not for him to see him cry. He rubbed the tears quick so the man didn't notice.

"There's a seal down there. Have you noticed it?" he asked.

"Yes," the man said, "it's always there."

"Do you think they look like dogs," Andrew said, still rubbing his eyes.

"Yes, a little," the man said. "Do you see its beautiful deep eyes?" said the man. "Those eyes see a whole world of its own down there, as you must use your eyes, boy, to see the world you live in up here and choose to live in it up here, to live in it and never give up."

"Yes, I suppose," said Andrew and sniffed hard and rubbed his face again.

As he packed up his gear, the man still sat there smoking his pipe. Andrew threw the rest of the left over squid to the seal at the bottom of the steps, and it landed with a sloppy loud slapping sound. The seal just looked up at him and he wasn't sure whether it would eat it or not once he had left.

As he walked away, he said, "Thank you for the conversation. I think I needed it maybe."

The man said, "Barnacles on the soul, boy, barnacles on the soul."

Getting back into the little town he noticed most lights were off. But the small pub still looked open, so he walked in. There was a young girl behind the bar looking at her phone.

"Are you still open?" he asked.

"Yes," she said, "but not for long."

"Can I have a pint of Guinness please?"

The girl stood up slowly, not being able to look at him but only into her phone.

Andrew sat in the corner. The place was empty, but had a log fire and it was cosy, he thought.

"Can I have another?" he asked.

"That was fast," said the girl.

"Life is fast," he replied. "Do you have digs?"

"Digs?" The girl looked up from her phone. "What does that mean?"

" A room or rooms to rent for people."

"You will have to ask my mam."

"Okay then," he said. "Is she around?"

"I'll go and get her," she replied and walked through a door.

A lady came from down the stairs and into the bar. She had curly black hair and a big pink jumper on. She looked old fashioned, he thought.

"My daughter said you were asking about a room."

"Yes, I've been fishing and I don't want to drive. It's late and I'm too tired." He smiled and she thought it was a nice smile and smiled back.

"Okay," she said. "We have a room and it's going to cost you forty pounds, and I need some identification because I have children here and can't just go giving strangers rooms without identification."

"I have a driving licence," he said.

"Okay," she replied, "but we are closing the bar soon, so do you want a last one?"

"Yes please," he said and smiled again. One more, he thought, you won't find answers at the bottom of the bottle, boy. He laughed at himself.

The next morning when he woke up, he sat on the end of the bed in his boxer shorts and looked out of the window. He opened it a little to let some air in. He lit a cigarette and then sat there for a few minutes and then reached back over and flicked his ash out of the small gap, noticing there was a small café down across the road from him. He enjoyed the silence, and then said to himself, barnacles on the soul. He threw his clothes on and packed up.

As he was about to walk into the café, an old lady was standing there. She looked down at his hand.

"Do you have a spare cigarette?" she asked.

"Yes," Andrew said and took a box out of his pocket and handed her one and then lit it for her.

"I'm not supposed to smoke, my daughter doesn't like me to, but I sneak one sometimes." She gave him a smile and a little wink.

"Do you work here?" he asked, looking at her red and white apron.

"Yes, my name is Joan." She took a last drag of the cigarette and flicked it with her skinny little fingers and it flew far across to the corner of the edge and dropped over and into the sea. She's done that for a long time, he thought. They walked inside and Andrew sat down.

"What can I get you, flower?" she said.

"Just a cup of tea with milk and two sugars please."

"Are you okay?" she asked.

"Yes, I will be I think."

"You been fishing?" she asked, looking at his rod bag and box.

"Yes, last night."

"Did you catch much?" she asked him.

"No, not a sausage."

They both smiled again.

"I did try to feed a seal though and had a nice chat to the lighthouse keeper and a few pints so it wasn't a total waste of a day."

She just smiled and giggled a little. "I think you're confused, dear, there hasn't been a lighthouse keeper here since I was a little girl, and I am 83 years old…"

Let's all breed thugs

Some parents are more concerned about their
child's self defence over their education.
Boxing gloves over books.
No wonder we can't dissolve violence
out of our primal instincts.
Even in a time of great science and technology.

I pushed her away

She never figured it out.
I was in love.

Hallelujah when chosen

The religious eccentrics that rub it in our faces
about God and how to act and live our lives
Make us feel pressured to admit belief.
And we class it as a form of brainwashing.
But everybody has had that one bad experience
that makes us look up and say
"Please get me through this and I promise
I will believe in you."

Green velvet eyes

Stabbed and bleeding, mugged and attacked, dragging himself through the forest,

Sanctuary is his only hope. The blood is endless, the fear is too real.

He can't believe what he is seeing… a cloak, a dark hooded cloak,

He believes it is his attacker come back to finish off the job, after all dead men can't speak.

"Leave me alone," he yells. "I have nothing. I had nothing then and I have nothing now."

The slow crunching footsteps in the snow is a sound every human being is familiar with and he now knows this is the end. A tall dark silent presence looks over him. This is not his attacker, he now realises, this is a fate much worse than that of the living. The thin hands and fingers rise up to the corners of the thick hood of the cloak.

"No," he begs. "I don't want to see. I know you are death and have come to take me."

As the hood comes down, a beautiful lady with green velvet eyes is staring silently at him. As she smiles and holds his cold hands with her warm caring gentle grip, she asks the question, "What was it you were scared to see? Was it a figure of bones instead of me? You have done nothing wrong in your life, this is what you have earned the right to see."

As she lifts him from the cold ground, they both walk calmly through and into the tallest oak tree…
We don't all get to see green velvet eyes.

Broken kings

A life of a drug dealer was the life he had chosen.
Selling drugs to the children
All the lives he had broken.
Dabbling with his own stash
he did not understand.
He had dealt with fate and been given a bad hand.

A burning sensation

A heartbeat is a silent sound
Just because you have been hurt
By someone
It does not always mean that it
Will be a constant crush
A heartbeat is a silent sound
Somebody can hold you and your body can freeze up
You know it is right
The emotion is there
A heartbeat is a silent sound
Fear of the unknown is embedded
In memory
But only a fool would look love in
The eyes and throw it away
But I can't shake it off
My back sweats, my eyes itch
Paranoia questions my future
A heartbeat is a silent sound
I will not be alone, I will fight
I will find
I will keep what nature was intended for us all
I will accept what is good for me
A heartbeat becomes
An orchestra of acceptance
And is filled with a dream
That I have made come true
In my self-belief.

Sidney and Stella

The sound of the birds woke him up, only he wouldn't open his eyes, not just because of the hangover, and not the brightness of the sun. Only because he knew it was the same shit about to repeat itself. Out of the corner of one half open eye, Sidney noticed a wood pigeon. It was moving its fat little body closer towards him. Almost lifting his hand to make it go away, he realised it wasn't doing any harm, and after all it never asked to be born, and that's the way he often felt about himself. Feeling there was no pain, no scratches or scrapes, no broken nose today. It would seem it couldn't have been a bad night.

As he sat up on the park bench, he looked back at the pigeon.

"Good morning."

The pigeon just carried on pecking at the ground. But that was okay, nobody really took any notice of him. So it was really quite normal.

"Let's see if we have anything left, shall we?"

The pigeon still pecking away, ignoring his very existence. Finding some change in his old coat pocket, the world seemed temporarily restored for the time being. It wasn't a lot but enough to take the edge off. Then after that life would be put back together again, and this time he really meant it. He found himself in the same store he always did, with nobody really noticing him, staring at the booze on the shelf. Didn't take long, in and out was the best way for him he found. As he approached the till, a lady was standing there. She looked sad, he thought, worn out and sad, and also buying booze.

"Excuse me, madam," he said. "We are in the middle of a lockdown. Covid-19 is everywhere. Where is your mask and gloves? And maybe you should get a little pie or a pickled egg to go with that bottle of alcoholic beverage."

She looked around and he smiled.

"I've already eaten. And anyway, that's what you look like, a pickled egg," and walked away.

He giggled and looked at the girl behind the counter, but she was not amused and only looked at him like he was something that blew into the store off the top of a rubbish skip.

As he left the store, he noticed she was over the road lighting a cigarette. He approached.

"They are no good for you, you know."

"People?" she replied.

"Yes, they are poisonous," he said.

That made them both grin.

"Bit early to get drunk," she said.

Sidney looked at the bottle of whisky. "Monkey see, monkey do," he replied. "I'm Sidney."

"Hi, I'm Stella."

"I have my own place," he said. "It's only small

if you would like company or just somewhere to drink. I'm not an axe murderer."

"How do I know that?" Stella replied.

"Look at me," he said and raised his eyebrows. "I'm more afraid of you."

She laughed. "Okay," she said.

Sidney's little apartment was so empty, a bed, a radio and empty bottles and cans, it was still clean. Just empty. But she didn't seem to mind. Sidney knew she had a drinking problem. It takes one to know one, he thought. But decided she still had too much pride for him to point it out.

"Take a seat, madam." He bowed down and she laughed again,

"Get some glasses," she said. "I'll pour."

Sidney only had one glass, so he gave her it and decided to use a cup.

"Do you only have one glass, Sid?"

"Yes, I like to pretend I am the Queen and it's tea," and then he did a silly wave.

"You're crazy," she said and poured the scotch. "What happened to you, Sid?" She knew it was a mood breaker but was curious.

"Life," he replied, "but let's not go there because drinking lifts me up or drops me down, and today my new blue eyed friend, I'd rather be up." He then smiled again, only this time he had pain in his eyes. And the smile seemed more unnatural and false.

"Can I ask you a question?" said Sidney. "How do you rate love?"

Stella thought for a moment and then looked into her glass of scotch. "I think love is the oldest game in the world, and it's the hardest one to play," and then took a slow sip.

"Let me ask you a question," she said.

"No," he replied, "so keep the ring in your pocket."

She laughed and he smiled at her.

"You're an idiot," she said and smiled back.

"You should stay the night," he said. "You on that chair and me on this chair, let's just drink. Maybe tomorrow you can leave your ruby slipper and I will come and find you again."

"Life is not a fairytale, Sid," she replied, and almost said he was no Prince Charming, but he was charming, and under that stubble he looked like a handsome man, and seemed to be a nice person, and had a nice smile, even if she did say it, so why kick a man when he's already down.

They drank for a while, and peacefully drifted to sleep.

In the morning Sidney woke up, and did the same thing he always did, only opened one eye. He realised he was alone, and Stella had left. Only this time his eyes watered with emotion, and he smiled like he hadn't smiled for a very long time, and turned over to sleep for a bit longer. Stella had left one of her shoes on the table...

Honesty and fear

A person who was working with me was having a lot of trouble in his life. I asked him what he was afraid of. He told me the only thing he was afraid of was being raped. I went quiet and then laughed. I then said, "No, you don't want that." It made me happy because it was so honest and direct and I think everything in life should be direct. His philosophy was that as long as he never got arse raped, then everything else would be okie dokie. Made me smile somebody confiding in me like that.

Mothers of the world

My mother works in an old people's home as a carer. An old lady who is very poorly with dementia and schizophrenia said to her, "When I finish eating these Weetabix I'm going to get up and give you a big cuddle, because you are always so so kind to me." She told me it made her job worth doing. That's how the NHS are.

Another time my mam met another elderly old lady who had been brought up by nuns and abused all her life. So my mother took her to Greggs one day and said, "You pick anything you want, it's your birthday."

The old lady said, "Is that a Cornish pasty?"

My mam said, "Yes, of course it is."

The lady said, "I haven't had one of those since I was a child. May I have one?"

My mam gave her it and said, "Go and sit down anywhere you like."

My mam got herself a vanilla slice and went and sat over next to the lady. The lady looked up at my mum and said, "Shall I begin?"

My mam was in shock and filled up inside and said, "Of course you bloody can, tuck in."

What kind of life could that lady have had to wait for permission to eat and only find freedom at such an old age?

Peacock dresses for the Chinese twins

The British Empire smuggled opium into China. No longer did the Chinese accept silver in exchange for tea, silk, and ceramics. So the empire began trading opium as a highly addictive bargaining chip. It was estimated that fifteen million Chinese citizens were addicted to opium from the poor to the wealthy by 1890…

As Mr Jardine walked from his ship and into the foggy streets of China, it didn't take him long to meet up with his business partner Ling.

"Hello Ling," he said.

"Hello Mr Jardine."

"Now stop that, Ling, I told you to call me William."

Ling bowed his head courteously and asked, "How is your beautiful wife?"

William grinned. "Ask her yourself. I have brought her with me on this trip and she is being taken to rest. It's been a long trip." William had a box and it had been wrapped as a gift with a big pink bow. "Tell me, Ling, how is your wife and your children? We have been doing business for a while now, Ling, and I would like to give you this gift as a token of our friendship, it's a gift for your daughters."

Ling looked surprised and took the gift. He then

looked down at William's boots. "You have new boots since last time, Mr Jardine."

"Yes, Ling, and your hair has grown longer since last time," and then they both laughed.

Late that night, Ling returned home and the children were sleeping peacefully with matching gowns. He watched over them as they slept, thinking of them as his very own angels. Also proud that his great grandfather had also had twins in the family and so he felt he had carried on a family tradition in a proud way. His wife was sleeping in the next room, so he walked in quietly as if not to awaken her, but she turned her head towards him.

"It's late," she said softly.

"It's business," he replied, "and I can't stay."

She looked down and asked what was in the box.

"A gift from Mr Jardine for the girls, now go back to sleep, my love."

Ling met back up with Mr Jardine and arranged a cargo of opium from him in return for large sacks of tea leaf and a quantity of silk. William had noticed Ling was sweating and getting irritated.

"Are you okay, my old friend?" he smiled.

Ling tried to smile and then asked if it was okay to leave as it had been a long day. "Goodnight, Mr

Jardine," and as he paused, he replied, "I mean, goodnight William." Ling then left.

But Mr Jardine was wise to the temptations of the streets and knew his nightcap was a desire and need for opium, and the ladies of the night. And as the dark misty opium slums sank into escaping reality, with their eyes wide shut, the rich men smiled with all of their friends as the twins danced in the moonlight wearing their new delightful, coloured peacock dresses.

Lost reflections

I had to confide in someone, and told them that I stand and talk to myself in the mirror, and does that mean I'm mad. They told me that if people never once looked into the mirror, and had to have a word with themselves, then they are mad.

The devil's smile

Walking alone in the garden of Eden, looking about without any reason, the sun was so bright, the trees were so green, it was the most beautiful thing that I'd ever seen. Suddenly I saw a figure come out from the trees.

"I am the devil. Come with me please, do not be afraid, show me no fear. I have something to show you, come over here."

He gave me a handful of slightly brown powder, asked me to taste it. As his voice got louder, I tried it. I liked it. I wanted some more. I had a craving like never before.

"Please help yourself," the devil said. "I think you should. It won't matter now, I've already poisoned your blood."

"Why did you do this? I thought you were my friend."

The devil just smiled and said, "Now your life will end."

"You think you have beaten me and taken my soul.

Leaving me to die here in this big black dark hole.

But now you will see me come back and fight.

I am going to slay you like a brave white knight.

We will see who is the winner at the end of each day.

I'm going to send your unnatural soul back to hell and there you will stay.

Read my poems, hear my voice get louder, the devil is on Earth, as a form of brown powder..."

Holding another man

My friend at the bar told me to tell our mutual
friend that he knows they have fallen out
And would I tell him he still loved him
I asked him
why can't you tell him yourself
and we are not on this earth forever
He got choked up and said
he will do it in the morning
He then asked me about the old days and said,
"Can we have them back?"
I answered
"No, we can't.
But we can keep hold of them in our hearts."
We then hugged
God bless him.

Clocks keep ticking

No, I shouted up
You can't have me
It's not time yet
But when it is
I've got some beautiful things to tell you.

Eating hope for breakfast

Sometimes I feel like a tea light
Them small round candles
I look in the bottom and
see a tiny flame is still burning
It's not a lot
but it's low
It refuses to die
But it's weak
I think the trick is to get a new one
Join the wicks
And keep it burning for all to see.

So it's not just me

There is a bit of Charles Bukowski in all of us.
There is hope.
shame.
love.
madness.
sadness.
nonsense.
fact.
belief.
disbelief.
reality.
falseness.
dignity and destruction.
But 'truth' is the one you must hold onto.
with both hands.

Upsetting the gods

She can never come back
I've cut away her wings
She stays down here
With me now
Your loss is
my true gain
But I know that you are crying
I can feel it
in the rain.

Miniature screwdrivers

If you have never had
Your heart broken
You will never
Feel the magic of it
being fixed.

Ocean of frost

I dreamt
I dreamt deeply
I'm sat in a social club
Everybody is in there with lots
of faces that I know
I'm drinking quietly but I need the toilet
I need to piss
Walking through touching people's shoulders
for them to look up
We smile at each other
As I walk to the toilet I see somebody working there
He sits with an old man
The old man is very drunk
He is telling the old man he is going to
throw him out if he doesn't leave
I sit down nearby
I watch quietly and know the younger man
He always did think he was a big man
but to me he is nothing
So I sit, watch and wait for him
to hurt the old man
So that I can hurt him a lot more
But as I watch this display of macho authority
He turns and sees me
He sees I'm not impressed
The gaze of madness I'm feeding him
Pushing my eyes deep into his

Squeezing what little soul he has left
Or is trying to attempt building
His face goes white
Eyes turning into little puppy dog eyes
"Will you help me carry him out?" he asked me
"What's he done to you?" I ask
"He's just too drunk
I've got to get him out, that's all"
I see the old man is falling off his chair
I know I want to help the old man
But not the other
"FUCK OFF, I'M ONLY GOING FOR A PISS"
I say
But I go over and grab the old man
He stands up all floppy
I walk him out through the pub
past everybody
He's thin and light and staring at me
He then looks over his shoulder at the mouthful of beer he has left
He is too drunk to stop me and go back
Even though he wants to
I'm only doing this so he doesn't get hurt
I worry how floppy he's going to get when the air hits him outside
When we do get outside, it's freezing
Blue ice
White fog
Patches of ice

Dirty grit imbedded
Some people walk past
Two men laugh
One of them takes off his own black woolly hat
He puts it on the old man's head
Over his eyes
Then laughs again
I pull it off with one hand
Still holding the man up
I slap the funny man across the face with it
It whips his eyes
He covers his face in shock
I whip him again and again until his silly friend takes him inside
The old man points across to an old car
It's a brown Robin Reliant
It looks so sad with frozen windows
I tell him he can't drive
He's too drunk and can't stand
I sit him down on the steps
I hold him
We don't speak
I don't know him
We just sit and look over at the sadness of the frost
The loneliness of the night
Then I wake up.

I asked her to hold me

Without passion from a woman.
Without a smile from a woman.
Without a stare from a woman.
Without birth from a woman.
Men are nothing…

Zombie apocalypse

Sometimes I think being crazy is a gift
I don't want this gift
When you see idiots walking about
Clueless
They sit next to you
They sit next to me 99% of the time
Always seeming to be happy with themselves
A mist of blankness
Sometimes trying to talk to me about fighting
I think that's what they believe I like
I hate violence
I hate cruelty
I hate football
I hate the norm
I hate them talking to me
I want them to go away
I'm too nice to just tell them
It burns me up inside
Makes me uncomfortable
Too much stress fills me up
I wish I was them sometimes
I'd not have to think too much
Thinking makes you crazy
These people do not have the ability to think
They are never going to be crazy
Just stupidity wrapped in flesh

Holding on to your honour

If you work hard and be kind
One day you will look up at the hospital ceiling
and know you did the right thing…

The Stag Inn

So furious
So angry
Sat with his fists on the table
looking over at us four
Me
Tommy
Stephen
and his brother Barry
Right, I said
I'm bored
Let's start a band
Let's call it
ROUND THE BENDIES
Oh great idea, said Stephen
Can I be the lead singer?
Yes, I agreed
But only if you wear a big top hat
Tommy, what can you play?
I can play the Didgeridoo, he said
Great
Barry, are you in?
Yes of course
What can you play though, Barry?
I play the pork chop flute
That will be wonderful, I said
And I can play the pokey eye
I then started poking my eyeball with my finger

and my eyeball went back and forth
back and forth
with the other eyeball staying still
We then all looked over at the man with the fists
Do you want to be in our band?
What instrument do you play?
YOU'RE ALL FUCKING MAD
He shouted
then left his drink
and stormed out of the pub
"NOW THAT'S POWER"

Souls of new beginnings

To all the loved ones
We have lost
We must keep on
Cherishing life
As a gift
To feel snow flakes
upon our faces
Running our fingers through the water
Looking up towards the sun
with its soothing gentleness
They will always be with us
Echoes in the silence
Memories in the wind
Whispers through the concrete
funny stories
Of disbelief.

Coffee with whisky in the staff room

In the early 80s when I was in primary school, I would sit alone and read Rodger Red Hat and Billy Blue Hat and just enjoy my own company and imagination. But they had a big board up in the classroom for everybody to see, teachers and all the children. On this board were all the children's names in a list going down, and along each child's name you would see a pointy gold or silver star for being good that week. But if you did okay you would get a green round dot sticker. But if you were bad or you struggled, you would get a red round dot sticker.

One day I stood and looked up and saw I had a full board of red dots all in a big long line, and as children we learn red is bad and means stop or danger, and all the children teased me and laughed at me.

I wasn't a bad child. I just struggled, and never really got noticed or was able to get the teacher's attention because they lacked patience for me. But we were children from the council estate, a place they didn't seem to come from, and probably never thought we would amount to anything. I looked up at the shiny stars of the other children, and wished they were mine, but never felt good enough to have just one.

It filled me with sadness. What adult would

choose that tactic to teach children, or is it a lesson to teach shame?

I was happy when they knocked that place down to rubble and nothing.

Smile with me

If you think you are losing your mind.
Just give in to its warm embrace.

Confusions of the stupid ones

Some people laugh at the idea, or sight,
or sound of poetry and stories.
I used to get angry at them, and feel silly.
But then memory reminds me they never
tried to learn to read or write.
A lot use dyslexia as an excuse,
but do not have it.
And I feel pity for the lack of ambition…

Moving through the swill

Just because the world around you looks and feels like you are in a pen, doesn't mean you have to act like a pig.

The Parmesan Bandits

I can hear them out there
I can hear the hate
Feel the hate
I can hear a loud motorbike from hell screeching
past the road and past my little flat
I can hear it speeding away
I think it's a scooter
I know who is riding it but
I don't know him by name
I've never even seen his face
But I know him more than he will ever know
himself in a million lifetimes
He is a teenager, late teens or maybe early twenties
He hates the world
He hates people, he hates himself
His mother used to go to the nightclubs long
before he was born
She hated staying in
His mother used to have one night stands
But it wasn't her fault,
she was young and having fun
She fell pregnant and the father didn't want to know
He was young also but selfish
and had no respect for her
He had been drunk and having fun also
It all boiled down to getting fixed up
When drunk nobody likes being lonely

Nobody likes to go home alone
So he's never had a father and he hated that
All he has is his eyes
His eyes that only see violence
His mother having boyfriend after boyfriend,
lover after lover
He hates her, he hates them
He rides that bike with anger
Has cocaine or weed or heroin between his balls
or up his arsehole in case the police pull him up
And he hates them too
Maybe he will run a child over
on the way to do the drop off
But that's okay because
everybody hates him anyway
So he hates them
He goes back home, slams the door
then opens the fridge
But there's not a lot in there
He hates that
His mother is in the kitchen with her best friend
They are smoking a joint
He argues with his mother about no food
She argues back because
he never gives her no money
Her friend joins in so he calls her a slag
He really wants to fuck her best friend
He probably will one day
He will fuck her hard and fast because he hates her

He's going to have the best car
The best clothes and the best house
And he says everybody is going to hate that
He has ten pairs of expensive trainers all lined up
All paid for with drug money
It makes him happy that all his other scumbag friends hate that
He wants to be like his master who he drops off the gear for
His master hates him
His master has no respect for him
Only pretends to like him
He is just a mule
Then he will go to jail and
his master will abandon him
He will be locked up
Told when to eat, when to sleep
His mother won't be there
He will hate that
He is a failure and will hate forever
He will probably crash his scooter and die
His short life will be a life of hate
His mother will cry and tell everybody in her path that it wasn't his fault
Her son wasn't like that
She will say everybody hated him then she will hate them
She will cry for weeks
Then put up a picture of him in the living room

He will be a little nice looking boy
He won't be the boy with the hoody up
and all the hate
Then she will sit in the kitchen with her best
friend and smoke another joint
She will look at her phone and talk to a stranger
who shows her a picture of his penis
She will send him an old picture of her vagina she
took in the bath that she keeps on her phone for
other strangers
He will ask to come round and she will say yes
They will watch Netflix
They will very quickly fuck in the living room
where the picture of her son is
He won't stay once they have finished
He will leave with an excuse
She hates that
Soon she will be pregnant again
The stranger will deny it
She will keep the baby and
get money off the government
When the baby gets older she will not read it books
Instead take it to kickboxing lessons
She will think the trainer is fit
and will tell her best friend
She wants her child to be able to fight
She will make it say "fuck off" and she and her
best friend will laugh with others
It will grow up as the man of the house once more

Driving fast down the road on his motorbike
with more drugs up his arsehole
The child might be a girl
So she will put makeup and skimpy clothes
on her at the age of ten
Then take lots of sexy selfies together
And then the girl will get her own phone and
house not far from her mam's
And have her very own TV and Netflix
Everybody will go round and have cocaine,
cider or lager in the kitchen
They will play music so loud the neighbours
will hate them
That will be fine because they hate the neighbours
The takeaways will keep coming
The delivery driver will hate going there
And the chain reaction will carry on
And on
With the endless labyrinth of blindness
Anger and hate.

Hunger for everything

What came first the chicken or the egg?
Nobody knows.
All we do know is humanity came to consume both.

Do you really want to suffer?

Human beings do not know sadness
until we are lying in bed by ourselves
Looking at the light through a crack
in the doorway
Breathing slow
And lonely
In the dark
Listening to the silent sound
of the radio

Open your eyes

I wish the whole world
Could see through my eyes
Violence would be obsolete
If these words
Warm your heart
That's nice
If not
It's only my opinion
It does not mean we are the same
Although if you are reading this
You already liked the title.
PAPER MOON 1973

The innocent ones

It really is an experience owning a dog
You can learn about your
Very own existence
Acknowledging them
Observing them
They start out as little pups
Weeping for the mother
You become her
You give all
As they grow and jump like springs
Playfulness
Energy is endless
They learn to settle and adapt
Gripping to your love and safety
Till one day you notice the eyes
You notice their eyes have changed
Eyes like deep lakes
You can't help thinking they should have been given more life
For their honesty
For the loyalty
Then they pass
Then we cry
But we should be happy
We have given them the best
Years of their lives.
R.I.P
Our children.

Self forgiveness is trapped in a fist of a bronze statue

Two weeks after my uncle died
He came to see me in a dream
I was sat in the corner of the box bedroom
The same place I gave him the heroin
twenty years ago
He walked through the wall from the left
Looked new, handsome and fresh
He told me to stop blaming myself
and it was his own choice and
that I have to carry on with life
He kept looking at the wall to the left
I cried and told him I was still sorry and asked
why he kept looking at the wall
He told me he wasn't allowed to stay
And I told him I missed him
And I needed him back
But he just walked back through the wall
and I woke up

Two weeks later I dreamt of him again
He was lying on my nana's sofa where I was
brought up
I saw him and he stood up but was silent
I cried again
Told him again I needed him
But he did not look into my eyes or speak

He just wrapped his arms around me and would
not let go until I woke
The third time he came into my dream
was only months later
He smiled and tried to talk about my life
But I broke again and cried
He just looked at me sad as if to say
"You still won't leave it and be happy"
then I woke up
I never saw him again
I love him
Too much.

To the stars and back

If it works out
I will tell her
I will marry her on the moon
And we will have a thousand babies
We will all love one another
Our souls will be entwined
Until my last breath leaves
My body
And awaits her
Until we are one again.

Stuff it

What a great way to make a living
they all thought
Such innocence and dedication
There's a lot of pride mixed into
this new job
Yes it can be cold
Yes there can be abuse
It is never nice when the new
Colleague gets kicked in his face
But you are all there to care
Mending the wounds
Helping him to recover
It's your first job but it also
Feels good to be self employed
You work for the old and the young
And all in between
To make a creation
A work of art
A team effort
As you all rub your cold fingers together
With pride and wage in pocket
Youth and contentment
Belongs to you
Yelling once more
"PENNY FOR THE GUY"

Stephen's freedom

Winkles winkles, he would pick them with a pin.
Women and beer or the odd double gin.
A man with no cares, is he a man who is lost.
Or is he a man who lives life at no cost.
How his pillow must be so gentle and so soft.
Such joy to the man who swung his fishing line.
He was my brother, my uncle
and was one of mine.
Watch his face, his smile is so clear.
He belongs to us and we hold him so dear…

Dementia

I was just ringing you, grandad,
to see if you are both okay
Yes, we are fine, Davie, are you okay?
Yes, just working all the time
That's good, Davie
Do you want to say hallo to nana?
Yes okay, pop her on then
Hello
Hi nana, are you okay?
Yes fine, who's this?
It's David
David?
Yes, David
Which one are you then?
I'm Julie's son, your daughter's oldest
But I lived with you all my life and
you made me toast in the morning
Then my dinner
Then cheese on toast at night with a cup of tea
You did everything for me
You kept me safe and warm
And loved me and I love you loads
Aaah that's nice, she says
Goodbye then, David
Okay nana, I love you loads, goodbye
I hang up and carry on working.

The love boat

I've whistled here
I've whistled there
I've breathed in the fumes
I've smelt the fresh air
I've watched how they smile
I've watched how they frowned
I've never kept my eyes stuck
On the ground
I've kissed the girl
I've made the mistakes
I've had some bruises up on my face
I've drank with the old
I've drank with the young
We've all been together
Sharing the same song.

A strange breed

Is it some kind of twisted right
That human beings can behave
any way that we like?
But only if the government
can decide all the rules
Is it some kind of twisted right
That there is one rule for us
But yet other rules for every single
creature on this planet?
Is it a twisted thought in my mind
That says if a dog bites a child
It must be put down immediately?
But yet if a so called human being
Molests a child and murders them
He or she get set meals everyday
And a roof over their heads
Can somebody please justify this to me
If the answer is they are sick
and need help
Then I'm sorry but I'm afraid
you do too.

The labourer

My very first job was probably my worst
I worked for my uncle who married into the family
My job was to mix a grey substance called Browning
I would mix twenty five bags into a plastic bath
with a garden rake
Back and forth
Back and forth with ribs and stomach tensing up
Then I would mix thirteen bags of plaster
They called it multi finish
They still call it that today
I was given ten pounds to do this
and worked ten hours
So figure that out
I was fifteen years old and
even then that was shit money
I knew it and so did he
I knew my nana had had a word
with my aunty to get me out of the house
So my uncle took me along
Maybe he wanted me to pack in and go home
Maybe cry to my nana
But I wasn't as soft as I looked
Not inside
So I never did
I was fast and strong
I also knew he knew I was good
but always pushed me harder and harder

No stopping
I would also carry a hundred six foot plaster
boards up a flight of stairs
one by one
Sweat would piss down my back and leak from
the back of my ears
But I still kept going, I would not break
The only problem was in them days
you never got an electric drill with a whisk
No, you got a metal bar with a
bicycle cog welded to it
It would have the cog on one end
And a handle on the other
But mine never had a handle even though they
were cheap to buy
I had to plunge it into a bucket of plaster
Up and down and in a circular motion
The bar would turn in my hands and it would
cause blisters all over every finger and my palms
I would stick my hands into the bag of plaster to
dry the blisters up
I would have to deal with them in the bath when
I got home and lie there in bed with my hands
spread out of the bed
throbbing thinking of the next day and
how I'll be able to use my hands again
I think the guilt crept in at some point and
I got twenty pounds a day
I showed my grandad my blisters and

explained you still get them wearing gloves
In fact it's worse but he just looked at me
then they tried giving me cream
The next morning I'd get in the van again
It was just like that
These days a teenager would get rushed to
hospital with hands full of blisters
or would have a nervous breakdown if they
couldn't be on their phone every twenty minutes
Different fucking gravy I was
People really worked then
One day me and my uncle got home
He lived at the bottom of the street
And I lived in the middle
It was Saturday and I had been paid
I just wanted to get a quick shower and get out
I wanted to have a drink
I needed to have a drink
The room light was off but the TV was on
The kitchen light was on, it looked bright
and I could smell cooking
It was corned beef stew
We always had that with brown sauce
We all loved it and with dumplings
I ran up the stairs and into the dark
Not giving myself time to switch on the light
I was in too much of a rush to drink
It was seven o'clock and I'd been to work since
eight that morning

The day was almost over
As I got to the top of the landing
There were four open doors
One was the bathroom and three were bedrooms
My nana was standing at her doorway
She was looking at me
It was pitch black but I could see her staring at me
Big white eyes on me
no noise at all
I walked over and looked at her
We were face to face
But it was so strange because she didn't seem to be breathing
It was so so silent and made me breathe low too
I said "WHAT IS WRONG WITH YOU?"
loudly
I then spread my arms and manoeuvred around her body, still looking at her big wide eyes on me like lost golf balls
I got to the light switch
Finding it with my blister fingers
But she was not there
She vanished into thin air
My stomach twisted and I went white
I ran down the stairs and into the room
There was my grandad on the sofa, snoring
I stormed into the kitchen and there she was, cooking
Were you just upstairs? I said

No, I'm cooking tea, David, she replied
I ran out of the house and down to my aunty's
I ran in and they all looked at me
What's wrong? my aunty said
I've just seen a fucking ghost, I think
I didn't go back home till I calmed down
I think it was my nana's mother
who had passed away not long before
She had been born in one of those
Romany gypsy wagons
So I guess she was one
When I met her as a child
she always smelt like roses
It was a strong smell
And I'd smelt that faint rose smell
when we were eye to eye
She had black curly hair and
big goggly eyes just like my nana
They were same height but she looked a little
smaller on the landing in the darkness.

Finding it

When you really love and cherish another
You both orgasm together at the same time
Putting your hands on each side of her face
Still both as one
Still connected
Both smiling and laughing at the power
You just shared
Sweat drips off your bodies
Eyes staring deep into each other's
Feeling both heartbeats
Your face falls into the side of her ear
You kiss her
Her hair is wet
You hold each other
In heat
In passion
This is the difference between love and lust
All else is simply
searching for that moment.

Broken records

I like bad boys
she told me
You like angry arseholes
who hit people
Sell drugs
Don't work
Drive fast cars
Loud mouthed
Fuck hard
Act hard
Then you get all dolled up
and visit them in prison
Fall for their lies
even though you know better
And then put a picture of yourself online
with a big black eye
Bust lip
Crying
I thought to myself
I'm a working man to the bone
Until I die
Don't let the tattoos fool you
I'm a teddy bear
It was nice meeting you
Goodbye
I said
It only takes one thing to put me off

I can't waste any more time finding love
Please better yourselves
You deserve so much more
than bad.

Puddles, olives, perfume and the purse

So there I was sat in Spain
In a villa with three Scousers
One of them was called Lee
He has a tattoo studio over in Birkenhead
Just over from Liverpool
I had been in a bad relationship
with a poisonous person
She just could not leave the pubs
She would finish work and go straight to the bar
I'd finish work and go do dinner
I loved to drink and still do
But not every day of the week
You've simply got to eat and have a nice home
This is how it went
Babe, I've made tea, it's six o'clock
Ow okay babe, ye I'll be home in twenty minutes
Okay babe, see you soon,
I've made lasagne and chips
Great babes
Babes, it's eight o'clock,
I'm trying to keep food warm
Ow okay, sorry ye I'll be home in a hour
Okay
Babes, it's twelve o'clock, where are you,
are you okay?
Ow babe, so so sorry
okay I'm walking home now

Babe, it's two o'clock in the morning
No answer, phones off
I'm still sitting there waiting for this alcoholic
What a bad person to be with
But you fall for it and it gets to the point
where you wonder if it's you
I packed as much as I could and went
and got the train
Hi Dave, where are you, babe?
I just got in, sorry, I got chatting
It's 3:30 in the morning and I'm on the train
Train, what?
Yes, I'm going home, dinner is in the bin,
goodbye
I deserve better, I told her
Anyway so I'm sat back at my home town
when I got a phone call
It was Lee who I was tattooing
for over Birkenhead
Do you want to pop over Spain and
talk about opening a studio?
Bring your tattoo equipment and
we will do a few over here
That meant me doing tattoos on his mates
Okay, I said
I'll pop over
So there we were and bouncing about
Having a laugh
All staying at Lee's villa he was so proud of

Funny how it was filled with pictures
of his mum and dad
It was obvious to me it was theirs until they
left him it and he had been going there
since they got it as a young boy
He had gotten to know the locals
and wanted to show he had friends
Lee was shy and quiet
Blushed a lot but was an okay lad, I had thought
I had made him plenty of money
working in his studio
Me doing all the work and giving him half
It was always the same in my life
The problem was he was always going
back and forth to Birkenhead
While I drank and waited for this big tattoo studio
idea of his with all this money he said he had
I'd sit at a place called the comic bar
It was loud and had comic strips all over the walls
Those two vikings you see
at the back of the newspapers
The little blond one and his fat red head mate
You know the ones
I'd decided to go see all the other bars
I went into a really nice quiet place
with nice quiet music
It was classy
I sat down and a lovely girl came over
and served me

I smiled and said hi and she smiled back saying hi
Are you English?
Yes, are you?
Yes, I'm from Birmingham, she said
She had moved there with her mother and brother
Her father was black and her mother was white
And what a beautiful little thing they had made
Her name was Chanel
Like the perfume, I said
Yes, she grinned
I was drinking whisky, it was nice and Chanel brought over some crisps and put them in a bowl
Then poured olives over them
Then squeezed lime all over
I had never had olives and I loved them
We sat and talked all night and ate olives
Then I saw her eyes change for a second
And looking at me different
Come here a minute, I told her and reached over and pulled her close
We kissed
A few days later I was sat enjoying a bottle of wine on her bed
When Lee rang me
Hey Dave, where the fuck are you?
I'm in love now, Lee
Speak later
Then I hung up

Lee has been bitching on about me not painting
his parents' villa while he was gone
Something for me to do, he had said
Oh I'd already had something to do, I thought
and I'd been putting in overtime
I was supposed to be there to be a tattoo artist
not a fucking decorator for free
I did overstay my welcome
But then I wasn't staying at the villa at all
He simply did not like me getting on with
all the locals and invited to all the parties
Having a sexy woman now twisted his little mind
After a while me and Chanel drifted apart
The reason seemed simple enough
all I would do is get drunk with her best friend
who was also called David
David was gay and there would be a gang of us
while Chanel worked
I think she had all the excitement out of me
and why not, she was young and beautiful
And I wasn't working there
or couldn't speak Spanish
It was okay though I still went to parties
and was at one one night
Nobody could speak English but we all smiled
and they would give me cuddles and drinks
You can see a lot about a person
in their eyes and smile
And I'd like to think they saw the niceness in me

So it was all sort of sign language talk
After they all left there was a big girl
She stood staring at me, smiling
I laughed and pointed my finger to the ceiling
She nodded and we went upstairs
She was a big girl and good looking
All she kept shouting was seeee seeee seeee
Afterwards she went downstairs for ages
Then when she came back to bed for more
Her breath smelt of Italian sausage
Greedy cow, I thought
where is mine?
I rolled over and slept
I can be selfish too
I was starving
The next day I was at a bar
when she brought her friend over to me
Her friend could speak a little English but
Sausage-lips could not
She said she want you to be her boyfriend
She informed me
How can we? I tried explaining
We can't communicate,
all she can say is seeee seeee seeee
They left
My money was drying up fast
I was doing the odd tattoo on the tourists in the villa
I'd give Lee half the money to stop him
complaining

People who are money mad like that
Makes them smile
I'd get drunk and people would ask me what I did
And next thing I knew I would be tattooing drunk
It paid and kept me over there
Lee kept on pissing on about me
not painting the villa
I told him I wasn't his fucking slave
He said he didn't want to throw me out
I took it as a last goodbye
We were really getting upset with each other
He then went back home
I said I'd go back in few days if it was okay
staying
I didn't want to go home with him and he
probably didn't want my company either
I had been partying and had women come over
and cuddle and kiss me when we were in bars
He had never spoke or had a woman all that time
we were there and he was single too
So no fucking studio then, Lee?
I told him
That's why I'm here, isn't it?
He realised he had been talking shit
I saw it in his face
It's okay, I said, next time you have
a business idea, keep me out of it
He left and went home
A couple of days later I was skint

but had just enough to get home
And a little bit extra
Outside there was this old broken down bull ring
You had to walk over it to get to the supermarket
It was a giant dent in the ground looking like a meteoroid had crashed into the earth
I walked in and got myself a bun
and a jar of olives
Olive sandwich
This situation was getting desperate
Even if I was not skint, the food over there was so bad, so stale smelling
Definitely not for me
The smell in there would make me go dizzy
I walked to the till
There was a lady there with a little boy
I waited behind them for my turn to be served
When they walked away I noticed the lady had left her purse on the counter
I grabbed it and ran after her
Excuse me, I shouted and held out the purse
She grabbed it and walked away
Bitch, I thought
You fucking bitch
That was no lady
There I was skint with a fat purse in my hand
and still doing the right thing
But it felt good not lowering myself as she did
Across the bull ring I went

I could see the light on in the villa
I'm going to miss that place, I thought
All those lovely hot soapy showers
With Chanel
While Lee was back home
Hot amazing sex in every room
Laughing, drinking on Lee's bed
Walking around naked
Heaven
Then half way there I heard a squeaky noise
I look down and there is this
black and white thing
Sticking its legs up out of a muddy hole
All pointing up
At first I thought, hmm rat
I looked closer and it was a tiny kitten
Wow, I thought and still drunk, I picked it up
And stuck it into my pocket full of mud
Then carried on to the villa
When getting back, I gave it a closer inspection
It was tiny and I think it just got trapped
Somehow
Lee had asked me to put some
English sausages in my suitcase
Me not knowing did it
and not knowing it was illegal to do that made
him a sneaky bastard
He had them defrosted in the fridge
and made me promise not to eat them

But now it was a celebration
I had saved a life and we were
both hungry lost souls
Filling the sink with warm water,
I gave the little fellow a bath
As Lee's English sausages sizzled away
We could both smell they were
going to be delicious
Puddles is your name, I said,
because that's where I found you
In one
In the morning I woke up and completely
forgot about it until I rolled over in Lee's bed
There was this tiny kitten smiling at me
Then it spread all its legs out at once
stretching on its back
Fuck
I shouted
What had I done?
I had to go home before Lee came back
I got dressed and saw the old cockney lady
next door
She was hanging washing out
We never spoke, she was a nosy old cow and had
lots of stories ready to tell Lee
She was itching for his return
Look, I told her,
I've saved a kitten and now I don't know
what to do with it

Do you like cats?
Maybe you can take care of it
Look how adorable it is
Does Lee know?
were her first words
No, he doesn't, I said
I saw in her eyes her and Lee had already been
taking about the disobedient slave and his chores
Just go and drop it in a bush, she said
Maybe on your fucking planet they
do things like that
But not on mine
Somebody should shot you in a fucking bush
She looked at me wide mouth
Fuck off, I said and slammed Lee's door
Lee had a mountain bike on top of the villa
and the slave used to go pick some food up
and cook it sometimes
Just to be nice
It was a shit bike but it worked okay
I travelled to the bars and cafés and all over the
place with a kitten in my pocket
I was out eight hours and nobody wanted Puddles
I gave up and took the bike back
Then sat in the comic bar
A bottle of water and a kitten
A man looked over at me, he was big
and had a ponytail in a knot
I could see he was dangerous

I could just sense it
Life can do that to you if you're not stupid
You can just feel things
Are you okay? he said in English
But he was not English
Not really, I replied
I need to get back home
But I found this kitten when I was drunk
And now I can't seem to find it a home
I'm stuck with it
My cat's just died, he said
I laughed
No really, he said and took out his wallet
and a photo of him and a cat
Give me a look at it, he said
I passed him Puddles
Cute, he said
I'll have it
I smiled
Thank you, I said
No, thank you, he said back
We spoke some more and he bought me a drink
I got to go, I said and shook his hand
Do you need a lift anywhere? he asked
Ye okay, I'm at a villa up the back roads
Ten minute walk
We went outside and got into
his Orange Lamborghini
I'm not into cars really but that was some car

We shook hands once more and
he left with Puddles and I came home
If Puddles is alive, he will be ten years old now
I often think about him when
I'm drunk sometimes
And I never did steal that purse.

Words that hurt, words that heal

I think that you are one of those people
who kills themselves
and nobody would have expected it
She said to me
What a horrible thing to say, I thought
It was horrible to hear
Because at the time it felt true
I stayed away after.
Ow my god, you are just too insatiable
She said and we laughed
She then left
I got my mop out and mopped the floor
Rug and chair
Everything was soaked
I felt good and manly
But lonely and unfulfilled at the same time
I stayed away after.
I don't think people are going
to see how talented you are
And different until you're gone, David
She told me
I took it as a compliment
She had seen the real me
We became friends
I see life as art
And art can be beautiful and ugly at the same time
But not be tied down
Only enjoyed

Enjoying the solitude

Letting thoughts dance through
My mind
Doing their own thing
Like a volcano building up pressure
Pencil sitting on notepad
Ready to put thoughts to paper
Rain is hitting my window from outside
In small silent waves
It's nice
Comforting
The dogs dream and twitch
I read my book
Kettle is boiling
Second hand is ticking
Valium makes my feet feel soft
The world seems quiet from here
Fox and hedgehog stick to their truce
Going their own ways
Surviving
Moving through streets
And into the darkness
With mystical eye.

Planet eyeball

I peak at the writing on the small
glass screen
We're all the new world inhabits
A person had written
FUCK THEM MY KIDS ONLY NEED ME
Then other messages pop up
ARE YOU OK?
Don't these people have other people's
phone numbers to talk?
And children need both parents
It's called stability
They must want to shame the other person,
I guess
How so very sad for the children
Another message reads
I LOVE MY CHILDREN,
THEY ARE MY WORLD
Has somebody doubted this about them?
That's not nice, is it?
They are your children
You are supposed to love them
It's called parenting
We believe you
It's okay, honest
Are they telling us this so we all better know
Or are they convincing themselves?
What has been going on in that house?

Another is calling the opposite sex, saying
YOU ARE ALL THE FUCKING SAME
This is not true at all
We are all different
That's what makes the world so complex
Have they gone mad?
Someone had put a secret message that seems
only the family members will understand
SOME FUCKING FAMILY I'VE GOT
Family is everything
Can't this person go round and work this silly
thing out, face to face?
Life is shorter by the day
Is love so distant?
Are we all so alone?
I throw my futuristic walkie talkie
on the table
Pick up my book and sit on the sofa
giving myself a million likes
In my mind
for doing so.

I have no spare change

As I pay my tax bill
They spit into the face of authority
It drips down into our mouths
Like toxic waste waterfalls
We are trying to protect the old
The damaged
The small weak children
They will not wear the mask
nor wash the hand
Walking around towns
like filthy tea cups
stained with dirt
Laziness and denial mixed
with conspiracy theories
Feeding us lies with bent
copper spoons
Wile we all sense death can come
to the doors at night
Yearning for an end to this madness
They laugh like wild hyenas
fighting over leftover meat
Walk slow like the tortoise
Brains like the sneaky fox
in the chicken pen
Talk about the life
they have never had
Overwhelming happiness

at extra benefits for alcoholism
Their graves
will never see a visitor
Nobody will care
not even their own
They will have given up long ago
robbed with no hope
Nothing they have done
will have contained achievement
They are the hole
in the shoe
The knife in the back
The bike that was taken
The baby food that was stolen
Put them in the skips
The wheelie bins
And let me pass
to where I am going
without getting upset
As I walk the paths
of broken slabs
Needles and piss
replace
the dandelions
and bumblebee.

The fly in the soup

Tramp is sleeping on concrete floor
using fist for pillow
Rich men scratch their ears
to show the Rolex
The schoolboy pops the ladybird
His friend runs to cry
Moon makes the mad men howl
in their cages
Promotion with handshake
and fine sports car
Addicts shoot up in bus station toilets
High paid football players
with egos like mountain tops
Low paid nurses
with bags under their eyes
The Eskimo slices the head from the seal
Dog fights dog
Cat chases mouse
What are we?
Where are we?
What will become of us?
Or do we even care?

A heart in a bed of nettles

Love is too far away
but solid friendships you can find
A cuddle
to be kind
A friend to unwind
The spikes can't be touched
only laughter and lust
It's beautiful and nice
My company is always here
So don't you ever think twice
But the heart can't be touched
It's broken too much
The damage has all been done
It will take time with someone
Your patience will fade
and I will have been wrong
I will lay in bed alone
until the guilt has all gone.

Pennies or sweets

What luxury it is today
to have pumpkins
As children we would carve
out turnips
How tricky it was to stop the
candle from falling down inside
Some carved potatoes
even carrots
Little evil faces
Such magical sight
and aroma
from the burning inside
Snot from noses
Fresh air in lungs
The world seemed so innocent
Families being together
Love surrounding the streets
Safety in numbers.

Spinning letters

I was twelve years old
I'd written my first poem
Then took it to the girl
down the road
Explaining I wanted her to
be my girlfriend
I was shy
Picking my moment
Holding it out to her
In an envelope
The wind blew and
stole it away
It flew and spun
frantically down the road
I chased after it
grabbing at it
Finally in my grip
I turned
She was gone
You see I've always
been a hopeless romantic
fool.

The vermin in the rain

The one really nice thing about a rainy day
Is that the scumbags don't like
To be in it
Maybe it's the natural beauty
that puts them off
The bailiffs must hate it
But it warms my heart and soul
knowing they are knocking at my door
All soaking wet
with no answer
I pat my dogs
That's the silly people
I say to them
Traffic wardens don't like the rain either
it makes their lonely sad little lives
even more depressing
and shallow
The weak don't like to get wet
Much like rodents
It's nice to not just write about
human beings sometimes.

Empty cabin

Our love burned
and roared
Like a wild
uncontrollable
fire
But you left me
And now I am all alone
I sit and stare
at cold dead ashes
Despising the logs
And curse my axe
for helping me
believe in the warmth.

Buckets of glitter

The whip cracked loudly
across his cheek
You silly little clown
you are but just weak
The circus girls laughed
and so did the freak
As he walked on by
the tear dropped down
from the makeup eye
Midnight came
lions prowled with fine mane
Oil lamps
flickered weak
The clown was silent
with vengeance to seek
The beast tamer slept deeply
as he walked in discreetly
Psychopathic and mean
stuffed a red nose in his mouth
not able to scream
Throat slashed slowly
gentle and clean
Sitting looking down
from the wooden stool
He whispered
don't take me
for such a blank fool.

Let's be realistic

Mary had a little lamb
It chased her through the snow
Her father came
and dragged it away
Then sliced it
head to toe.

Shopping list

Four prawn rings
A lemon
Ice cream
Eggs
Butter
Asparagus
Pizza
Rosé wine
Lemonade
Salmon
Olives
Lime
Ready salted crisps
Pepperoni
Pigs in blankets
Is there anything else
you want?
She asked
Yes
What?
YOU x

Cream

So I said to myself
one day
You are one cool cat

Digging in the mud

Life is about
finding yourself
I never want to find myself
I'm having too much fun
in the search.

I can't cope

Stephen
Stephen
O my sweet Stephen
I hate you so much
I cry to the ladies
instead of the lust
You have left a big hole
that cannot be filled
One day we will cry
into each other's eyes
Our love is a must
But you have left me to rust.

Lights out

Isn't it strange
when people
sit in pubs
Talking proudly
about having been
to prison
They can't
be that proud
They ask you
to buy them
a pint.

Hitchhiker's guide to the funny farm

When doing this
you come to realise that not
many normal people
will pick you up
And that old thumb trick
is a myth
It never works
Especially when you've got your head down
The way to do it is to find a nice
big piece of cardboard
and a marker pen
You hold up the sign
indicating which way you are heading
A name of a place
A kind message under the name
Please help
something like that
Then you would hold it up
and look at the drivers in the face
Mainly the truck drivers
They would be so tired that a good
conversation would keep them awake
Trucks were best
They would have really cosy chairs
tea and coffee
Sometimes food
And some would have little dogs travelling

with them as companions
I always liked that
It made me feel they were good people
and compassionate
One man picked me up wearing
lipstick and eye shadow
Painted nails and high heels
He never said a lot
And I never stayed in there long
Here will do, I said
Thanks
You would walk up the slip roads
and the police would pick you up
and take you back to the start of it
So then you would start walking
up it again
You could be a hour walking
and now have to start all over again
There was me and a lad named Ron
Ron knew a girl who was a nurse
and a friend
She invited us up to Cardiff in Wales
Late at night after walking for hours
a car pulled over
I jumped in first with my backpack
Just before Ron got in
the police pulled up behind the car
and I looked at them from
out of the back window

As they got out
I heard Ron say to them
Sorry, we know we aren't supposed
to be on the slip roads
Then I saw the copper point at the car
and say
No, we want him
who is driving that car
I turned, looked at the driver
There was this man with a black woolly hat
It had been stitched on one half
to fit his head
He had brown curly hair
coming out all the sides
Had on a black T-shirt
His arms were solid muscle
Tight
Cut
with veins all over
He looked around and his face shocked me
His nose was all smashed in
He had scars everywhere
That's it
I thought
He's an escaped lunatic
He's going to take off with me in the car
The police ended up just giving him
a short lecture
about picking up hitchhikers

And he just apologised
Ron then got in and we set off
My mind eased a little
But I kept looking how rough and
Fucked up this man looked
My name is Ernie
He told us
Hi, I'm David
Hi, I'm Ron
He started really speeding down the short roads
Then he kept looking back
Then built up speed 80
Then looked back again
Then more speed 90
THEY ARE AFTER ME YOU KNOW
Who? I asked
With my arsehole in my mouth
THEM BASTARDS
THEM FUCKING FREEMASONS
THREE YEARS I'VE BEEN RUNNING NOW
This was bad, I thought
trying to find my seatbelt
Ron was laughing nervously
But there was nothing funny about this situation
That was obvious
MILK AND BISCUITS, he shouted
What you on about? I asked
UNDER THE SEAT
MILK AND BISCUITS

I reached down and sure enough
there was a bag with packs of them
and a load of milk
I passed him them and he munched away
and took massive gulps of the milk
while still going 90mph
THIS IS ALL I HAVE EATEN AND DRANK
FOR THREE FUCKING YEARS
THE BASTARDS
THEY WON'T LET ME SETTLE
But why would somebody be chasing you?
I had to ask
His story was this
He had been left a lot of money
Family inheritance
And had joined the Freemasons
He was also happily married
But having fallen out over a large amount
of money he owed
and could not eventually pay
they had kidnapped him
took him to an abandoned house
In the middle of nowhere
Locked him in a bedroom for two weeks
with boarded up windows
They had sleep interfered with him
I asked what that meant
He said they wait until you are asleep
and then they talk to you through the walls

from the next room
Telling you things to do
Then they let him go
He remembered being very dizzy and confused
He had gone home
Took out a big long bread knife
from the kitchen drawer
Stuck it into his wife's stomach
But his wife was wearing a big thick coat
and the knife had bent
Not being able to penetrate her
She ran screaming
They then locked him up in a psychiatric ward
Not being able to get out
And nobody believing that
he had been told to do it
Or even being kidnapped
His wife left him
I listened to this and sipped sneakily
at my bottle of Jack Daniels
Listening to all of this
Still speeding like a mad man
He carried on his story
They eventually let him out
and he got himself a small quiet flat
Then one day he was boiling some eggs
in a pan in the kitchen
When a large man with a bald head
walked in with a hammer

Smashed it over Ernie's head
He went down
But got back up in shock
Grabbed the pan of boiling water with the eggs
still bouncing about in it
and threw it into the man's face
The man screamed
and Ernie ran out of his flat and into his car
He claimed he had been running
ever since that day
I BET YOU THINK I'M LYING TO YOU
I BET YOU THINK I'M CRAZY
He said to me
Nope, never said that, my friend, I replied
HERE FEEL THE BACK OF MY HEAD
Nope, I'm fine thanks
PLEASE PLEASE PLEASE FEEL IT
He wasn't going to take no for an answer
I put my hand under his hat
and all the curly wild hair
Gave it a little rub
Sure enough a big dent
About the size of a hammer imprint
Okay, I said, that's it
I really have to piss
Stop the car so I can piss
No reply
Ernie, my friend, stop the fucking car
before I piss myself

He finally stopped
I got out first
Then Ron leaped out
We ran like fuck
Not looking back
We were in the middle of nowhere
But we found a graveyard
with two wooden benches facing each other
Ron slept across on one
And I sat looking over
Finishing off my last bit of JD
I looked up at the stars
They were beautiful
But I couldn't help but think
Was there any truth in Ernie's story?
And if so
What an incredible one
And what a poor lost soul
This is a true story
I never hitchhiked again
after that.

Unwanted games

I don't know why I think so deeply
about hurt and heartache
I need to shake it off but I can't
My mind is too deep
I feel like I'm going to put together
a giant jigsaw puzzle
Knowing there is going to be lots of pieces
missing at the end
That would make the whole thing meaningless
Taking up so much time as I age
Leaving me alone
I think I'm scared of being left alone

The adventures of Captain Onion

The first time I saw this I was
seven years old
I was walking to the shop
to get my nana five pounds of potatoes
I was walking behind an old man
who had problems
He walked round talking
to his invisible friend beside him
Some used to say it was his brother who died
But Bobby still walked along as if they were
still in conversation
Bobby would be gabbing on and on
and then sometimes a big argument
would explode
Bobby kept repeating the same thing over
and over again
A pint of milk
A loaf of bread
A newspaper
And then again and again
A pint of milk
A loaf of bread
A newspaper
On and on
When we got to the shop
The lady said hallo Bobby
What can I get you?

He paused for a couple of seconds
and then said
I can't remember
Then walked out
Then there was a tall man in front of me
He was very thin and had really big ears
His ears were really blue
His nose was really big and also blue
I could not figure out why he was so cold
It was summer time and hot
I walked home with the potatoes
When it was dinner time
I sat with my grandad and told him all about
Bobby and the blue man
What did the man buy?
He asked me
A big bottle of brown cider, I said
He was pickled, my grandad told me
With a mouth full of food
Pickled?
Yes, David, pickled
Then he pointed at the jar of onions
Look David, if you have too much booze
instead of blood
You pickle like them onions
I went to bed that night
Not being able to sleep
Wow, I saw a man that wanted to
be a pickled onion
I thought
It was so fascinating to me.

Stop saying that

How are you doing?
I'm alright
You've got to be, don't you.
NO YOU DON'T HAVE TO
JUST BE ALRIGHT
YOU CAN BE ANYTHING
THAT YOU WANT TO BE
ANYTHING
THIS WORLD IS YOURS
OURS
FIND IT
EMBRACE IT
GRAB IT BY ITS THROAT
AND SCREAM IN ITS FACE
LOOK AT ME
YOU CRAZY BITCH.

A tight grip

One man sits to the left of me
One man sits to the right
The one on the left speaks of violence
And how he likes to fight
The one on the right is tired
From working night and day
I only shake one hand as I leave
The one who's earned his pay.

Future through a monster's eye

The young prince could no longer live
with the suicide of his one and only
true love
As he climbed naked
to the dead rocks
way up high
Wind sliced through his short blond hair
Skin so cold and so blue
Fingertips as cold as the rocks themselves
Teeth and jaw as tight as a bear's trap
Looking down with such
sadness and loss
Rain whipping at his thin naked skin
No more tears
There were no more to give
He threw himself with such fury
and velocity
Seeming to glide in slow motion
Peace was welcoming him
with open arms
Hoping that the Gods would embrace him
Eyes closed
Time was to stop
Peace was to begin
Rocks drew closer
The giant kraken emerged from the soul
of the deep sea

Waving its tentacles high and proud
With loud slap and wetness
the young prince now stuck to the suckers
chest to stomach
It slowly brings his cold grey brittle body forward
Water shoots from its mighty fins
Holding him closer to an overwhelmingly
large golden eye
with a green diamond shape in its centre
The prince raises his soaked head
to look at his reflection inside
He is now an old worn out king
with long grey hair
Long grey beard
Fine clothing and large crown
The king looks back
into his young eyes
proudly
His queen reaches over and holds the king's hand
She smiles as she looks across to the prince
Hanging there watching
She is also old and grey
But also still beautiful
She blows him a kiss with her free hand
and looks back towards her king
They are in love
The kraken lays the prince's body
gently onto the sandy shore
nearby
And swam away with
great might.

Sobriety

I just got sick of seeing life through a foggy lens.

Cuckoo

She is a schizophrenic
You say
And you are still going round?
he asked
Yes, she is so amazing
I replied

Think about it

Suicide is easy
Life is the tricky part.

Endless friendships

I don't know how you approach it.
But having good friends in life
really warms my heart.

Strong seeds

How far do we bend the branch
Until we feel the snap.
All depends on the strength of the tree.